Side Tab Mini Slouch

Design by Salena Baca

Skill Level

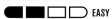 **EASY**

Finished Sizes

Instructions given fit child; changes for teen and adult are in [ ].

Finished Measurement

Length: 8 inches *(child)* [9 inches *(teen)*, 10 inches *(adult)*]

Materials

- Plymouth Yarn Encore Worsted medium (worsted) weight acrylic/wool yarn (3½ oz/200 yds/100g per skein):
  1 [1, 2] skein(s) #466 quarry
- Size H/8/5mm crochet hook or size needed to obtain gauge
- Tapestry needle
- 1-inch button: 1

Need help? **Stitch Guide.com** ILLUSTRATED GUIDES HOW-TO VIDEOS

Gauge

14 hdc = 4 inches;
8 rows = 4 inches

Pattern Notes

Chain-2 at beginning of round counts as first half double crochet unless otherwise stated.

Join with slip stitch as indicated unless otherwise stated.

Hat

Band

Row 1: Ch 73 [81, 89], sc in 2nd ch from hook, sc in each rem ch across, turn. *(72 [80, 88] sc)*

Row 2: Ch 1, sc in each st across, turn.

Row 3: Ch 1, sc in each of first 2 sts, ch 3, sk next 3 sts *(buttonhole made)*, sc in each rem st across, turn.

Row 4: Ch 1, sc in each st across, working 3 sc in ch-3 sp.

Row 5: Rep row 2. Do not fasten off.

Body

Rnd 6: Now working in rnds, **ch 2** *(see Pattern Notes)*, hdc in same st, [sk next st, 2 hdc in next st] 32 [36, 40] times, leaving last 7 sts unworked, **join** *(see Pattern Notes)* in top of beg ch-2. *(66 [74, 82] hdc)*

Rnds 7–19 [7–21, 7–23]: Ch 2, hdc in same st, [sk next st, 2 hdc in next st] 32 [36, 40] times, join in top of beg ch-2.

Last rnd: Ch 2, [sk next st, hdc in next st] 32 [36, 40] times, join in top of beg ch-2. Leaving long end, fasten off. Weave long end through sts of last rnd, pull to close top of hat. Secure end.

Brim Edging

Working in ends of rows and in starting ch on opposite side of row 1, join with sc in end of row 5 on Band opposite buttonhole, sc in each st around Band, working 3 sc in each corner. Fasten off.

Finishing

Sew button on Band opposite buttonhole. ●

Easy Beanie

Design by Carolyn Pfeifer

Skill Level

 **EASY**

Finished Sizes

Instructions given fit child; changes for teen and adult are in [ ].

Finished Measurement

Circumference: 17 inches *(child)* [19 inches *(teen)*, 21 inches *(adult)*]

Materials

- Plymouth Yarn Jeannee Worsted medium (worsted) weight cotton/acrylic yarn (1¾ oz/110 yds/50g per skein):
    2 skeins #05 heather

4 MEDIUM

- Size H/8/5mm crochet hook or size needed to obtain gauge
- Tapestry needle

Gauge

9 pattern sts = 2 inches; 6 rows = 2 inches

Pattern Note

Hat is worked in turned rows.

Stitch Pattern

Row 1: *Working in **front lp** *(see Stitch Guide)*, sc in next st, working in **back lp** *(see Stitch Guide)*, dc in same st, sk next st, rep from * across.

Row 2: *Working in front lp, sc in next dc, working in back lp, sc in same st, sk next sc, rep from * across.

Hat

Row 1 (RS): Ch 31 [35, 39], sc in 2nd ch from hook and in each ch across, turn. *(30 [34, 38] sts)*

Row 2: Ch 1, working in back lps, sc in each of first 5 [6, 6] sts, working in both lps, work row 1 of Stitch Pattern over next 18 [20, 24] sts, working in back lps, sc in each of next 7 [8, 8] sts, turn.

Row 3: Ch 1, working in back lps, sc in each of first 7 [8, 8] sts, working in both lps, work row 2 of Stitch Pattern over next 18 [20, 24] sts, working in back lps, sc in each of next 5 [6, 6] sts, turn.

Rows 4 & 5: Rep rows 2 and 3.

Row 6: Ch 1, working in back lps, sc in each of first 5 [6, 6] sts, working in front lps, sc in each of next 18 [20, 24] sts, working in back lps, sc in each of next 7 [8, 8] sts, turn.

Row 7: Ch 1, working in back lps, sc in each of first 7 [8, 8] sts, working in front lps, sc in each of next 18 [20, 24] sts, working in back lps, sc in each of next 5 [6, 6] sts, turn.

Rows 8–11: [Rep rows 6 and 7] twice.

Size Small Only
Rows 12 & 13: Rep rows 6 and 7.

All Sizes
Rows 14–19 [12–17, 12–17]: [Rep rows 2 and 3] 3 times.

Rows 20–27 [18–23, 18–23]: [Rep rows 6 and 7] 4 [3, 3] times.

Rep rows 14–27 [12–23, 12–23] until piece measures 17 [19, 21] inches from beg. Leaving long tail for sewing, fasten off.

Finishing
Fold piece in half. Using long tail, sew back seam. Weave rem tail through ends of rows at top of Hat, pull to close. Secure end. ●

Aviator Hat

Design by Salena Baca

Skill Level

◼◼◻◻ EASY

Finished Sizes

Instructions given fit child; changes for teen and adult are in [ ].

Finished Measurement

Length: 7½ inches *(child)* [8 inches *(teen)*, 8½ inches *(adult)*], excluding Earflaps

Materials

- Plymouth Yarn Encore Worsted medium (worsted) weight acrylic/wool yarn (3½ oz/200 yds/100g per skein):
  1 skein each #240 taupe, #459 lagoon, #462 woodbine, #451 green gremlin and #450 green
- Size I/9/5.5mm crochet hook or size needed to obtain gauge
- Tapestry needle

Gauge

13 dc = 4 inches; 7 rows = 4 inches

Pattern Notes

Change color in last stitch of round.

Join with slip stitch as indicated unless otherwise stated.

Chain-2 at beginning of round counts as first double crochet unless otherwise stated.

Stripe Color Sequence

Child Hat: First 6 rnds taupe, 1 rnd lagoon, 1 rnd woodbine, 1 rnd green gremlin, 1 rnd green, 2 rnds taupe.

Teen Hat: First 7 rnds taupe, 1 rnd lagoon, 1 rnd woodbine, 1 rnd green gremlin, 1 rnd green, 2 rnds taupe.

Adult Hat: First 8 rnds taupe, 1 rnd lagoon, 1 rnd woodbine, 1 rnd green gremlin, 1 rnd green, 2 rnds taupe.

Hat

Getting started: Refer to Stripe Color Sequence throughout Hat.

Rnd 1: Make **slip ring** *(see illustration)*, 12 dc in ring, **join** *(see Pattern Notes)* in first dc. *(12 dc)*

Rnd 2: Ch 1, 2 dc in each st around, join in first dc. *(24 dc)*

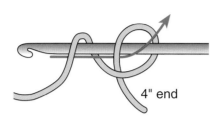

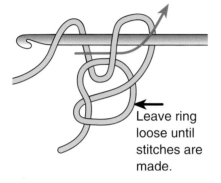

4" end

Leave ring loose until stitches are made.

Slip Ring

Rnd 3: Ch 1, dc in first st, 2 dc in next st, [dc in next st, 2 dc in next st] around, join in first dc. *(36 dc)*

Rnd 4: Ch 1, dc in each of first 2 sts, 2 dc in next st, [dc in each of next 2 sts, 2 dc in next st] around, join in first dc. *(48 dc)*

Rnd 5: Ch 1, dc in each of first 3 sts, 2 dc in next st, [dc in each of next 3 sts, 2 dc in next st] around, join in first dc. *(60 dc)*

Size Child Only

Rnd 6: Ch 1, dc in each st around, join in first dc.

Sizes Teen & Adult Only

Rnd [6]: Ch 1, dc in each of first [9, 4] sts, 2 dc in next st, [dc in each of next [4, 9] sts, 2 dc in next st] around, join in first dc. *([66, 72] dc)*

All Sizes

Rnds 7–12 [7–13, 7–14]: Ch 1, dc in each st around referring to Stripe Color Sequence, join in first dc. Do not fasten off.

Right Earflap

Row 1 (RS): Now working in rows, **ch 2** *(see Pattern Notes)*, sk next st, dc in each of the next 7 [9, 9] sts, sk next st, dc in next st, leaving rem sts unworked, turn. *(9 [11, 11] dc)*

Row 2: Ch 1, sc in each st across, turn.

Row 3: Ch 2, sk next st, dc in each of the next 5 [7, 7] sts, sk next st, dc in last st, turn. *(7 [9, 9] dc)*

Row 4: Rep row 2.

Row 5: Ch 2, sk next st, dc in each of next 3 [5, 5] sts, sk next st, dc in last st, turn. *(5 [7, 7] dc)*

Row 6: Rep row 2.

Row 7: Ch 2, sk next st, dc in each of next 1 [3, 3] st(s), sk next st, dc in last st, turn. *(3 [5, 5] dc)*

Size Child Only

Fasten off.

Sizes Teen & Adult Only

Row [8]: Rep row 2.

Row [9]: Ch 2, sk next st, dc in next st, sk next st, dc in last st. Fasten off. *([3, 3] dc)*

Left Earflap

All Sizes

Row 1: With RS facing, sk next 21 [27, 29] sts on rnd 12 [13, 14] on Hat after Right Earflap, join in next st on rnd 12 [13, 14], rep row 1 for Right Earflap.

Rows 2–7 [2–9, 2–9]: Rep rows 2–7 [2–9, 2–9] of Right Earflap.

Edging

Rnd 1: Working in sts and ends of rows, join taupe in center back of Hat between Right and Left Earflaps, sc in each st around Hat and Earflaps, working 3 sc in each dc end row on Earflaps, join in first sc. Fasten off. ●

Mini Slouch Hat

Design by Salena Baca

Skill Level

■■■□ INTERMEDIATE

Finished Sizes

Instructions given fit child; changes for teen and adult are in [ ].

Finished Measurement

Length: 8 inches *(child)* [10 inches *(teen)*, 12 inches *(adult)*]

Materials

- Plymouth Yarn Encore Tweed medium (worsted) weight acrylic/wool/rayon yarn (3½ oz/200 yds/100g per skein):
  1 [2, 2] skein(s) #1237 granola
- Size H/8/5mm crochet hook or size needed to obtain gauge
- Tapestry needle
- ¾-inch buttons: 3

4 MEDIUM

Gauge

14 hdc = 4 inches;
7 rows = 4 inches

Pattern Notes

Ribbing section is worked first from side to side, and then stitches for Body are worked in ends of Ribbing rows.

Chain-3 at beginning of round does not count as first stitch.

Join with slip stitch as indicated unless otherwise stated.

Special Stitch

Cluster (cl): Holding back last lp of each st on hook, 4 dc as indicated, yo, pull through 5 lps on hook.

Hat

Ribbing

Row 1: Ch 9 [11, 13], hdc in 2nd ch from hook and in each ch across, turn. *(8 [10, 12] hdc)*

Rows 2–38 [2–42, 2–46]: Ch 1, working in **back lps** *(see Stitch Guide)*, hdc in each st across, turn. Do not fasten off.

Body

Getting started: Hold Ribbing in circle with first two rows behind last two rows.

Rnd 1: Now working in rnds, **ch 3** *(see Pattern Notes)*, working in rnds and in ends of rows on Ribbing and through both thicknesses where Ribbing overlaps, [tr in end of next row, **cl** *(see Special Stitch)* in end of next row] 18 [20, 22] times, **join** *(see Pattern Notes)* in first st. *(18 [20,22] tr, 18 [20,22] cls, total of 36 [40,44] sts)*

Rnds 2–9 [2–10, 2–11]: Ch 3, [**fptr**—*see Stitch Guide* around tr on last rnd, cl in next cl] 18 [20, 22] times, join in first st.

Last rnd: Ch 3, fptr around each fptr on last rnd, join in first st. Leaving long end, fasten off. *(18 [20, 22] fptr)*

Finishing

Weave long end through sts on last rnd, pull to close. Secure end. Sew buttons along edge of Ribbing to close ends. ●

Unisex Beanie

Design by Salena Baca

Skill Level

 INTERMEDIATE

Finished Sizes

Instructions given fit child; changes for teen and adult are in [ ].

Finished Measurement

Length: 7½ inches *(child)* [8 inches *(teen)*, 8½ inches *(adult)*]

Materials

- Plymouth Yarn Encore Tweed medium (worsted) weight acrylic/wool/rayon yarn (3½ oz/200 yds/100g per skein):
  - 1 skein each #T520 dark grey and #T217 black
- Size I/9/5.5mm crochet hook or size needed to obtain gauge
- Tapestry needle

Gauge

14 hdc = 4 inches;
7 rows = 4 inches

Pattern Note

Join with slip stitch as indicated unless otherwise stated.

Special Stitch

Extended single crochet (esc): Insert hook in st as indicated in instructions, pull up a lp, yo, pull through 1 lp on hook, yo, pull through both lps on hook.

Hat

Rnd 1: Make **slip ring** *(see illustration)*, 10 hdc in ring, **join** *(see Pattern Note)* in first hdc. *(10 hdc)*

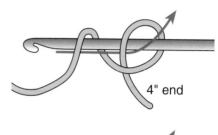

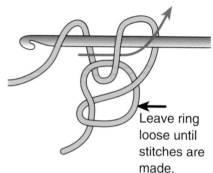

4" end

Leave ring loose until stitches are made.

Slip Ring

Rnd 2: Ch 1, 2 hdc in each st around, join in first st. *(20 hdc)*

Rnd 3: Ch 1, hdc in first st, 2 hdc in next st, *hdc in next st, 2 hdc in next st, rep from * around, join in first st. *(30 hdc)*

Rnd 4: Ch 1, hdc in each of first 2 sts, 2 hdc in next st, *hdc in each of next 2 sts, 2 hdc in next st, rep from * around, join in first st. *(40 hdc)*

Rnd 5: Ch 1, hdc in each of first 3 sts, 2 hdc in next st, *hdc in each of next 3 sts, 2 hdc in next st, rep from * around, join in first st. *(50 hdc)*

Rnd 6: Ch 1, hdc in each of first 4 sts, 2 hdc in next st, *hdc in each of next 4 sts, 2 hdc in next st, rep from * around, join in first st. *(60 hdc)*

Sizes Child & Adult Only

Rnd 7: Ch 1, hdc in each of first 19 [3] sts, 2 hdc in next st, *hdc in each of next 19 [3] sts, 2 hdc in next st, rep from * around, join in first st. *(63 [75] sts)*

Size Teen Only

Rnd [7]: Ch 1, hdc in each of first [5] sts, 2 hdc in next st, *hdc in each of next [5] sts, 2 hdc in next st, rep from * around to last 6 sts, hdc in each of last 6 sts, join in first st. *([69] sts)*

All Sizes

Rnd 8: Ch 1, sk first st, dc in each of next 2 sts, working in front of dc sts just made, **esc** *(see Special Stitch)* in skipped st, *sk next st, dc in each of next 2 sts, working in front of dc sts just made, esc in skipped st, rep from * around, join in first dc. *(63, [69, 75) sts)*

Rnd 9: Ch 1, hdc in each st around, join in first hdc.

Rnds 10–14 [10–14, 10–16]: Rep rnds 8 and 9 alternately, changing to black in last st of last row. Fasten off dark grey.

Rnd 15 [16, 17]: With black, ch 1, sc in each st around.

Rnd 16 [17, 18]: Ch 1, **bphdc** *(see Stitch Guide)* around each of first 2 sts, **fphdc** *(see Stitch Guide)* around next st, *bphdc around each of next 2 sts, fphdc around next st, rep from * around, join in first st.

Rnd 17 [18, 19]: Ch 1, bpsc around each of first 2 sts, fpsc around next st, *bpsc around each of next 2 sts, fpsc around next st, rep from * around, join in first st. Fasten off. ●

Summer Hat

Design by Rebecca Huber

Skill Level

 EASY

Finished Size

One size fits most

Finished Measurement

Length: 8½ inches

Materials

- Plymouth Yarn Encore Chunky Colorspun bulky (chunky) weight acrylic/wool yarn (3½ oz/ 143 yds/100g per skein):
    1 skein #7357 tan/cream variegated
- Plymouth Yarn Europa Tweed bulky (chunky) weight wool/acrylic/rayon yarn (1¾ oz/ 87 yds/50g per skein):
    1 skein #04 neutral
- Size K/10½/6.5mm crochet hook or size needed to obtain gauge
- Size N/P–15/10mm crochet hook
- Tapestry needle

Gauge

Size K hook: Rnds 1 and 2 = 4 inches

Pattern Note

Join with slip stitch as indicated unless otherwise stated.

Hat

Rnd 1: With size K hook and tan/cream variegated, ch 4, **join** (see Pattern Note) in first ch to form ring, [dc, ch 1] 12 times in ring. (12 dc, 12 ch-1 sps)

Rnd 2: [Dc, ch 1, dc, ch 1] in each ch-1 sp around. (24 dc, 24 ch-1 sps)

Rnd 3: [Dc, ch 1] in each ch-1 sp around.

Rnd 4: *[Dc, ch 1] in each of next 4 ch-1 sps**, [dc, ch 1, dc, ch 1] in next ch-1 sp, rep from * around, ending last rep at **. (28 dc, 28 ch-1 sps)

Rnd 5: Rep rnd 3.

Rnd 6: Rep rnd 4, ending last rep with [dc, ch 1] in each of last 3 ch-1 sps. (33 dc, 33 ch-1 sps)

Rnds 7–9: Rep rnd 3.

Rnd 10: Sc in each dc and each ch-1 sp around. (66 sc)

Brim

Rnd 11: Sc in each of next 3 sc, 2 sc in next sc, rep from * around to last 2 sc, sc in each of last 2 sc. (82 sc)

Rnds 12–17: Sc in each sc around. At end of rnd 17, fasten off.

Tie

With size P hook and holding 2 strands of neutral tog, make a ch 28–30 inches long, leaving a long tail on each end. Fasten off. Weave Tie through ch-1 sps on rnd 9 and tie in bow. Tie additional strands of neutral around center of bow, if desired. ●

Cozy Ribbed Hat

Design by Margaret Hubert

Skill Level

 INTERMEDIATE

Finished Size

One size fits most

Finished Measurement

Circumference: 22¾ inches, with brim turned up

Materials

- Plymouth Yarn Gina medium (worsted) weight wool yarn (1¾ oz/109 yds/50g per skein): 2 skeins #06 gray/green/purple variegated
- Size I/9/5.5mm crochet hook or size needed to obtain gauge
- Tapestry needle
- ⅞-inch buttons: 2
- Tapestry needle

 4 MEDIUM

Gauge

14 sc = 4 inches;
6 rows = 2 inches

Pattern Notes

Hat is worked in turned rows with short row shaping.

Work in back loops unless otherwise stated.

Hat

Row 1: Ch 41, sc in 2nd ch from hook and in each ch across, turn. *(40 sc)*

Row 2: Ch 1, working in **back lps** *(see Stitch Guide and Pattern Notes)*, sc in first sc, sc in each of next 31 sc, turn, leaving rem 8 sc unworked. *(32 sc)*

Row 3: Ch 1, sc in first sc, sc in each of next 31 sc, turn.

Row 4: Ch 1, sc in first sc, sc in each of next 31 sc, sc in next 8 unworked sc on row 2, turn. *(40 sc)*

Row 5: Ch 1, sc in first sc, sc in each of next 39 sc, turn.

Next rows: [Rep rows 2–5 consecutively] 19 times. Fasten off.

Finishing

Thread a tapestry needle with a 30-inch strand of yarn, gather top of hat to shape crown. Secure end. Working through back loops of foundation ch and last row worked, sew back seam, leaving a 3-inch opening at bottom. Turn brim up 3 inches, fasten in place with 2 buttons. ●

Newsboy Hat

Design by Rebecca Huber

Skill Level

 INTERMEDIATE

Finished Sizes

Instructions given fit small/medium; changes for large are in [ ].

Materials

- Plymouth Yarn Jeannee Worsted medium (worsted) weight cotton/ acrylic yarn (1¾ oz/110 yds/ 50g per skein):
    3 skeins #10 faded blue
- Size I/9/5.5mm crochet hook or size needed to obtain gauge
- Tapestry needle

Gauge

Rnds 1–9 = 4 inches diameter

Pattern Notes

Hat is worked in continuous rounds; do not turn or join unless otherwise stated. Mark first stitch of round.

Wrong side of Hat is used as right side for texture.

Visor is worked in turned rows.

Work loosely when working front post single crochet and slip stitches to maintain size. Alternatively, use a larger hook size to work these stitches.

Join with slip stitch as indicated unless otherwise stated.

Hat

Rnd 1: Ch 2, work 7 sc in 2nd ch from hook. *(7 sc)*

Rnd 2: Work 2 sc in each sc around. *(14 sc)*

Rnd 3: [Sc in next sc, 2 sc in next sc] around. *(21 sc)*

Rnd 4: [2 sc in next sc, sc in each of next 2 sc] around. *(28 sc)*

Rnd 5: [Sc in each of next 3 sc, 2 sc in next sc] around. *(35 sc)*

Rnd 6: Sc in next sc, [2 sc in next sc, sc in each of next 4 sc] 6 times, sc in each of next 3 sc, 2 sc in last sc. *(42 sc)*

Rnd 7: Sc in each sc around.

Rnd 8: [2 sc in next sc, sc in each of next 5 sc] around. *(49 sc)*

Rnd 9: Rep rnd 7.

Rnd 10: Sc in each of next 2 sc, [2 sc in next sc, sc in each of next 6 sc] 6 times, sc in each of next 4 sc, 2 sc in last sc. *(56 sc)*

Rnd 11: [Sc in each of next 7 sc, 2 sc in next sc] around. *(63 sc)*

Rnd 12: Sc in each of next 3 sc, [2 sc in next sc, sc in each of next 8 sc] 6 times, sc in each of next 5 sc, 2 sc in last sc. *(70 sc)*

Rnd 13: Rep rnd 7.

Rnd 14: [2 sc in next sc, sc in each of next 9 sc] around. *(77 sc)*

Rnd 15: Rep rnd 7.

Rnd 16: Sc in each of next 4 sc, [2 sc in next sc, sc in each of next 10 sc] 6 times, sc in each of next 6 sc, 2 sc in last sc. *(84 sc)*

Rnd 17: [Sc in each of next 11 sc, 2 sc in next sc] around. *(91 sc)*

Rnd 18: Rep rnd 7.

Rnd 19: Sc in each of next 5 sc, [2 sc in next sc, sc in each of next 12 sc] 6 times, sc in each of next 7 sc, 2 sc in last sc. *(98 sc)*

Rnd 20: Rep rnd 7.

Rnd 21: [Sc in each of next 13 sc, 2 sc in next sc] around. *(105 sc)*

Rnd 22: Sc in each of next 3 sc, [2 sc in next sc, sc in each of next 14 sc] 6 times, sc in each of next 11 sc, 2 sc in last sc. *(112 sc)*

Rnds 23 & 24: Rep rnd 7.

Rnd 25: Sc in each of next 5 sc, [**sc dec** *(see Stitch Guide)* in next 2 sc, sc in each of next 14 sc] 6 times, sc in each of next 9 sc, sc dec in last 2 sts. *(105 sts)*

Rnd 26: Rep rnd 7.

Rnd 27: [Sc in each of next 13 sts, sc dec in next 2 sts] around. *(98 sts)*

Rnd 28: Sc in each of next 4 sts, [sc dec in next 2 sts, sc in each of next 12 sts] 6 times, sc in each of next 8 sts, sc dec in last 2 sts. *(91 sts)*

Rnd 29: Rep rnd 7.

Rnd 30: [Sc dec in next 2 sts, sc in each of next 11 sts] around. *(84 sts)*

Rnd 31: Sc in each of next 5 sts, [sc dec in next 2 sts, sc in each of next 10 sts] 6 times, sc in each of next 5 sts, sc dec in last 2 sts. *(77 sts)*

Rnd 32: Rep rnd 7.

Rnd 33: Sc in each of next 3 sts, [sc dec in next 2 sts, sc in each of next 9 sts] 6 times, sc in each of next 6 sts, sc dec in last 2 sts. *(70 sts)*

Size Small/Medium Only

Rnd 34: [Sc in each of next 8 sts, sc dec in next 2 sts] around. *(63 sts)*

Size Large Only
Rnd [34]: Rep rnd 7.

All Sizes
Rnd 35: Rep rnd 7.

Rnd 36: Ch 1, turn, working loosely, **fpsc** *(see Stitch Guide)* around each sc around, **join** *(see Pattern Notes)* in first st. *(63 [70] fpsc)*

Rnd 37: Ch 1, turn, sc in each fpsc around, do not turn.

Rnd 38: Working loosely, sl st in each sc around, join in first st. Fasten off.

Visor
Row 1: Ch 34, sc in 2nd ch from hook and in each ch across, turn. *(33 sc)*

Row 2: Ch 1, sc dec in first 2 sts, [ch 1, sk next sc, sc in next sc] across to last 3 sts, ch 1, sk next sc, sc dec in last 2 sc, turn. *(16 sts, 15 ch-1 sps)*

Row 3: Ch 1, sc dec in first st and first ch-1 sp, [ch 1, sk next sc, sc in next ch-1 sp] across to last 3 sts, ch 1, sk next st, sc dec in last ch-1 sp and last st, turn. *(15 sts, 14 ch-1 sps)*

Rows 4–10: [Rep row 3] 7 times. Fasten off at end of row 10. *(8 sts, 7 ch-1 sps)*

Align opposite side of foundation ch on Visor with center front of rnd 38 on Hat, pin in place. Working through both thicknesses, join in first st, sl st in each st across Visor. Fasten off.

Edging
Working in sts, ch-1 sps and ends of rows along Visor edge, join in center back of Hat, sc in each st around entire Hat and Visor, join in first sc. Fasten off. ●

Modish Crochet Hats is published by Annie's, 306 East Parr Road, Berne, IN 46711. Printed in USA. Copyright © 2014, 2015 Annie's. All rights reserved. This publication may not be reproduced in part or in whole without written permission from the publisher.

RETAIL STORES: If you would like to carry this publication or any other Annie's publication, visit AnniesWSL.com.

Every effort has been made to ensure that the instructions in this publication are complete and accurate. We cannot, however, take responsibility for human error, typographical mistakes or variations in individual work. Please visit AnniesCustomerService.com to check for pattern updates.

ISBN: 978-1-57367-557-4

4 5 6 7 8 9

STITCH GUIDE

STITCH ABBREVIATIONS

beg .... begin/begins/beginning
bpdc .... back post double crochet
bpsc .... back post single crochet
bptr .... back post treble crochet
CC .... contrasting color
ch(s) ....chain(s)
ch- .... refers to chain or space
    previously made (i.e., ch-1 space)
ch sp(s) .... chain space(s)
cl(s) ....cluster(s)
cm .... centimeter(s)
dc .... double crochet (singular/plural)
dc dec .... double crochet 2 or more
    stitches together, as indicated
dec .... decrease/decreases/decreasing
dtr .... double treble crochet
ext ....extended
fpdc .... front post double crochet
fpsc .... front post single crochet
fptr .... front post treble crochet
g ....gram(s)
hdc .... half double crochet
hdc dec .... half double crochet 2 or more
    stitches together, as indicated
inc .... increase/increases/increasing
lp(s) ....loop(s)
MC ....main color
mm ....millimeter(s)
oz ....ounce(s)
pc ....popcorn(s)
rem .... remain/remains/remaining
rep(s) ....repeat(s)
rnd(s) ....round(s)
RS ....right side
sc .... single crochet (singular/plural)
sc dec .... single crochet 2 or more
    stitches together, as indicated
sk .... skip/skipped/skipping
sl st(s) .... slip stitch(es)
sp(s) .... space(s)/spaced
st(s) .... stitch(es)
tog .... together
tr .... treble crochet
trtr ....triple treble
WS .... wrong side
yd(s) ....yard(s)
yo .... yarn over

YARN CONVERSION

OUNCES TO GRAMS		GRAMS TO OUNCES	
1	28.4	25	⅞
2	56.7	40	1⅔
3	85.0	50	1¾
4	113.4	100	3½

UNITED STATES		UNITED KINGDOM
sl st (slip stitch)	=	sc (single crochet)
sc (single crochet)	=	dc (double crochet)
hdc (half double crochet)	=	htr (half treble crochet)
dc (double crochet)	=	tr (treble crochet)
tr (treble crochet)	=	dtr (double treble crochet)
dtr (double treble crochet)	=	ttr (triple treble crochet)
skip	=	miss

Single crochet decrease (sc dec):
(Insert hook, yo, draw lp through) in each of the sts indicated, yo, draw through all lps on hook.

Example of 2-sc dec

Half double crochet decrease (hdc dec):
(Yo, insert hook, yo, draw lp through) in each of the sts indicated, yo, draw through all lps on hook.

Example of 2-hdc dec

Reverse single crochet (reverse sc):
Ch 1, sk first st, working from left to right, insert hook in next st from front to back, draw up lp on hook, yo and draw through both lps on hook.

Chain (ch):
Yo, pull through lp on hook.

Single crochet (sc):
Insert hook in st, yo, pull through st, yo, pull through both lps on hook.

Double crochet (dc):
Yo, insert hook in st, yo, pull through st, [yo, pull through 2 lps] twice.

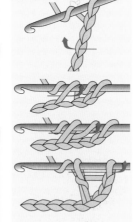

Double crochet decrease (dc dec):
(Yo, insert hook, yo, draw lp through, yo, draw through 2 lps on hook) in each of the sts indicated, yo, draw through all lps on hook.

Example of 2-dc dec

Front loop (front lp) Back loop (back lp)

Front Loop   Back Loop

Front post stitch (fp): Back post stitch (bp):
When working post st, insert hook from right to left around post of st on previous row.

Back   Front

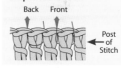

Post of Stitch

Half double crochet (hdc):
Yo, insert hook in st, yo, pull through st, yo, pull through all 3 lps on hook.

Double treble crochet (dtr):
Yo 3 times, insert hook in st, yo, pull through st, [yo, pull through 2 lps] 4 times.

Treble crochet decrease (tr dec):
Holding back last lp of each st, tr in each of the sts indicated, yo, pull through all lps on hook.

Example of 2-tr dec

Slip stitch (sl st):
Insert hook in st, pull through both lps on hook.

Chain color change (ch color change)
Yo with new color, draw through last lp on hook.

Double crochet color change (dc color change)
Drop first color, yo with new color, draw through last 2 lps of st.

Treble crochet (tr):
Yo twice, insert hook in st, yo, pull through st, [yo, pull through 2 lps] 3 times.